# BEYOND WORDS

## MASTERING THE POWER OF COMMUNICATION TO UNLOCK WEALTH

# TABLE OF CONTENTS

# INTRODUCTION

## The Power of Communication

In today's fast-paced, noisy world, communication is more essential than ever before. From the constant stream of notifications to the overflow of digital content, it seems as though we're bombarded with messages at every turn. Amid all this noise, the ability to communicate effectively is no longer just a useful skill—it's a superpower. Whether you're pitching a new client, leading a team, or scaling your business, clear and intentional communication is the foundation of success.

Effective communication goes far beyond simply speaking words; it's about making an impact, forging relationships, and driving results. The ability to convey your message with clarity and purpose can set you apart in a world where attention spans are fleeting, and messages often get lost in the shuffle. When you communicate in a way that resonates with your audience, you create opportunities for growth, trust, and collaboration. In short, your communication becomes the engine that propels your business forward.

This book is your guide to bridging the gap between speaking and real communication. It's not enough to just say the words—real communication is about making a genuine connection, sharing your message in a way that is both clear and compelling, and using the power of your words to move your business and your audience toward action. The tools, strategies, and mindset shift you'll encounter in the following chapters are designed to help you refine your communication skills, craft messages that stand out, and unlock new levels of success in your business.

## The Noise of the World and the Need for Real Communication

We live in an age where communication is constantly evolving. We have more ways to connect with others than ever before—social media, email, text messages, webinars, podcasts, video calls—and yet, despite these advancements, the art of meaningful communication often feels like it's getting lost in the shuffle. In a world filled with distractions, it's easy to get caught up in the noise and forget what it truly means to connect with others on a deep level.

This disconnect is especially felt in the business world, where the noise can sometimes drown out the message. Entrepreneurs, business owners, and leaders are tasked with cutting through that noise to reach their target audience, convey their value, and build lasting relationships. This is where real communication comes in. Real communication isn't about competing with the noise; it's about standing out with a message that is clear, purposeful, and relevant to the people you want to reach.

The first step in mastering real communication is understanding that the key to success isn't just about what you say—it's about how you say it. When you speak with intention and purpose, your words carry weight. They have the power to inspire action, foster trust, and spark connections that drive business growth. In this book, you'll discover how to harness the power of your voice and your words to not only speak but to truly communicate in a way that leads to results.

## Communication is the Bridge to Connection

Communication is the bridge that connects people. Whether you're trying to win over a new client, motivate your team, or make a lasting impression at a speaking engagement, your ability to connect with others is the key to achieving success. When you communicate effectively, you are not just conveying information; you are building relationships and creating an environment in which collaboration and trust can thrive.

For many business owners and entrepreneurs, the struggle lies in bridging the gap between speaking and true connection. We may know what we want to say, but it's easy to fall into the trap of speaking without really engaging the listener. Perhaps you're presenting a product, service, or idea, but if your message doesn't connect with your audience on an emotional or intellectual level, it's unlikely to spark the interest or response you're hoping for. The ability to engage, inspire, and move others to action hinges on your capacity to communicate in a way that is meaningful to them.

Real communication begins with a deep understanding of your audience. It's about knowing what they care about, what challenges they face, and how your message can meet their needs. Once you understand your audience, you can craft your message in a way that speaks directly to them, creates a sense of relevance, and builds the trust needed for them to take the next step with you. By focusing on clarity, empathy, and engagement, you can transform simple words into a powerful tool for building connections and driving action.

## The Role of Clarity in Communication

Clarity is at the core of effective communication. If your message is unclear, no matter how well-intentioned, it will fall flat. Clear communication doesn't just make it easier for people to understand what you're saying—it also makes it easier for them to take action based on what they've heard. In business, the ability to articulate your message clearly can be the difference between making a sale and losing a potential customer.

Clarity starts with focus. You need to know exactly what it is you want to say and, just as importantly, why it matters. When you're clear on your message and the value it brings, you can deliver it in a way that is both succinct and compelling. This is one of the first lessons you'll learn in this book: how to distill your message to its essence, eliminating unnecessary complexity and making it easy for your audience to connect with and understand.

The value of clarity extends beyond just the words you choose. It also applies to how you structure your message, how you present your ideas, and how you engage with your audience. Whether you're crafting an email, giving a speech, or writing a marketing copy, clarity ensures that your audience knows exactly what you're offering and how it benefits them. As you move through the chapters, you'll learn how to sharpen your message, remove distractions, and communicate with precision.

## Intentional Communication Creates Action

While clarity is critical, it's not enough to simply be understood—you must also inspire action. Whether you're aiming to persuade a client to sign a contract, motivate your team to achieve a goal, or drive customers to purchase your product, your communication must inspire action. Intentional communication goes beyond delivering information; it's about crafting a message that moves your audience to do something—whether it's making a decision, taking the next step, or engaging with your brand in a meaningful way.

The power of intentional communication lies in its ability to influence behavior. In business, this translates to higher conversion rates, stronger customer loyalty, and a more engaged and motivated team. Every message you send is an opportunity to move people closer to your desired outcome, and the strategies you'll learn in this book will help you develop the skills needed to make those opportunities count.

## What to Expect from This Book

In the chapters ahead, you will discover actionable strategies, powerful techniques, and mindset shifts designed to refine your communication skills and take your business to the next level. From crafting a compelling message to using storytelling to inspire, from understanding the psychology of communication to overcoming the barriers that often hold us back, this book will provide you with the tools you need to communicate with clarity, connection, and purpose.

Each chapter builds on the last, guiding you through the process of becoming a more effective communicator, and ultimately, a more successful business owner.

You will learn how to:

- Develop a core message that resonates with your audience.
- Use storytelling to connect on an emotional level.

- Leverage the psychology of communication to inspire action.
- Align your message across different platforms.
- Overcome common barriers to effective communication, including fear and self-doubt.
- Cultivate daily habits for continuous improvement in your communication skills.

By the end of this book, you'll not only be able to speak more clearly and persuasively—you'll have the ability to create real, lasting connections that propel your business forward.

## The Transformation Starts Now

Communication is the bedrock of every successful business, and mastering it is the key to unlocking your full potential. Whether you're just starting out or looking to refine your skills, the tools and insights shared in this book will help you become a more powerful, more effective communicator.

The transformation doesn't happen overnight, but each step you take toward becoming a better communicator will bring you closer to your goals. By putting the strategies into practice, you will be able to speak with purpose, connect with your audience, and ultimately lead your business to new heights.

The power of real communication is within your grasp. It's time to stop speaking and start connecting. The transformation starts now.

# CHAPTER 1

# Speaking vs. Communicating

As a business owner or entrepreneur, you're no stranger to speaking. Every day, you engage in conversations with employees, clients, vendors, and colleagues. You write emails, pitch ideas, and share your expertise with audiences large and small. But have you ever stopped to ask yourself, "Am I truly communicating?"

The difference between speaking and communicating is both subtle and profound. Speaking is the act of producing words—it's about what *you* are saying. Communication, on the other hand, is about what the *listener* is understanding. It goes beyond the surface of language to ensure your message is clear, meaningful, and actionable. In this chapter, we'll explore why this distinction is critical and how mastering real communication lays the foundation for your success.

## The Problem with "Just Speaking"

Speaking is easy. You think of the words, you say them, and you move on. But how often do you stop to consider whether those words landed with your audience? Did they understand your point? Were they engaged, inspired, or compelled to take action?

Many of us assume that because we're articulate, we're effective communicators. But being able to string together eloquent sentences doesn't necessarily mean you're connecting with your audience. Imagine a CEO presenting a new strategic initiative to their team. They deliver a lengthy, data-heavy speech filled with jargon and industry buzzwords. Despite their expertise, the employees leave the room confused and disengaged. The problem wasn't the speaker's intelligence—it was their inability to communicate in a way that resonated with their audience.

Speaking without true communication often leads to:

- **Misunderstanding**: Your audience doesn't grasp your message.
- **Disengagement**: They lose interest because your words don't connect.
- **Inaction**: They don't know what to do next, so they do nothing.

For entrepreneurs, these pitfalls can be costly. A confusing pitch could mean losing a potential investor. A disengaging sales presentation might cost you a client. And unclear instructions to your team can lead to wasted time and resources.

## What Is Real Communication?

Real communication is intentional. It's the process of creating understanding and inspiring action. It requires you to step outside of yourself and consider your audience's perspective. What do they need to hear? How can you deliver your message in a way that makes sense to them?

Real communication is built on three key pillars:

1. **Connection**: At its core, communication is about building relationships. People are more likely to listen to you if they feel seen, heard, and understood. Connection creates trust, which is the foundation of influence.
2. **Clarity**: A clear message is an effective message. If your audience has to work too hard to decipher what you're saying, they'll tune out. Clarity ensures that your message is easy to understand and impossible to ignore.
3. **Action**: Communication isn't just about exchanging ideas—it's about driving outcomes. Whether you want your audience

to buy your product, support your initiative, or simply remember your message, you need to guide them toward the next step.

## The Science Behind Communication

The distinction between speaking and communicating is deeply rooted in how the human brain processes information. Research shows that people are more likely to retain information when it is:

- **Relevant**: Does it address their needs or solve their problems?
- **Organized**: Is it presented in a logical, easy-to-follow structure?
- **Engaging**: Does it evoke emotion or spark curiosity?

When you're simply speaking, you're relying on your audience to do the heavy lifting of decoding and interpreting your words. But when you focus on communication, you take responsibility for making your message as digestible as possible.

Consider the famous quote by George Bernard Shaw: "The single biggest problem in communication is the illusion that it has taken place." Too often, we assume that because we've said something, it's been understood. Real communication ensures that assumption doesn't lead to lost opportunities.

## Examples of Speaking vs. Communicating

Let's break down the difference with a few examples:

1. **Sales Pitch**
    - **Speaking**: "Our software has advanced algorithms, real-time processing, and multi-platform integration."
    - **Communicating**: "Our software helps you save time and increase productivity by streamlining your workflows across all devices."

2. **Team Meeting**
    - **Speaking**: "We need to improve our efficiency by 15% this quarter."
    - **Communicating**: "If we reduce the time spent on repetitive tasks, we can save an additional 5 hours per week, allowing us to hit our 15% efficiency goal."

3. **Marketing Message**
   - **Speaking**: "We're the leading provider of XYZ services in the industry."
   - **Communicating**: "We help businesses like yours grow faster by delivering XYZ services with proven results."

In each example, the shift from speaking to communicating involves tailoring the message to the audience's perspective, focusing on outcomes, and making the message easy to understand.

## Why Connection, Clarity, and Action Matter

When you prioritize connection, clarity, and action, your message becomes more than just words—it becomes a tool for transformation.

- **Connection**: Helps you build trust and rapport, whether you're speaking to a client, employee, or investor.
- **Clarity**: Ensures your audience knows exactly what you're saying and why it matters to them.
- **Action**: Drives results by giving your audience a clear path forward.

These three elements are not optional—they're essential. Without them, your message will likely fall flat, no matter how passionate or knowledgeable you are.

## Steps to Transition from Speaking to Communicating

To close this chapter, let's look at some practical steps you can take to transition from just speaking to truly communicating:

1. **Start with the End in Mind**: Before you speak, ask yourself, "What do I want my audience to think, feel, or do as a result of this message?" Let your goal guide your communication.
2. **Know Your Audience**: Take the time to understand who you're speaking to. What are their challenges, priorities, and goals?
3. **Simplify Your Message**: Strip away jargon and focus on the essence of what you want to say. Clarity beats complexity every time.
4. **Engage Emotionally**: Use stories, analogies, or examples that resonate with your audience's experiences.

5. **Invite Feedback**: Communication is a two-way street. Encourage your audience to ask questions, share their thoughts, or clarify their understanding.

## Conclusion

Speaking and communicating may seem like interchangeable terms, but they couldn't be more different. Speaking is about you; communication is about your audience. When you learn to communicate with connection, clarity, and action, your words become a powerful tool for building relationships, inspiring trust, and driving results.

In the next chapter, we'll dive into the cornerstone of real communication: clarity. You'll learn how to craft a core message that resonates with your audience and ensures your voice stands out in a crowded marketplace.

# CHAPTER 2

## Clarity is King – Crafting a Core Message That Resonates

Clarity. It's a word we often hear, yet one that's elusive for many business owners and entrepreneurs. In a world saturated with information and distractions, clarity has become the currency of influence. Without it, your message is just noise in a crowded marketplace. With it, your voice rises above the competition, capturing the attention of your audience and leaving a lasting impression.

In this chapter, we'll explore why clarity is the cornerstone of effective communication, how to eliminate the clutter in your messaging, and the steps to crafting a core message that not only resonates but also drives action.

### The Importance of Clarity

Let's start with a simple truth: If people don't understand your message, they won't act on it.

Imagine walking into a store and asking for directions to a specific product, only to have the salesperson give you a long-winded explanation filled with unnecessary details. You'd likely leave the conversation feeling frustrated or confused. The same principle applies in business communication. When your message is unclear, you lose your audience's attention—and, often, their trust.

Clarity is about more than just simplicity; it's about precision. It's ensuring that every word you say has a purpose and contributes to your audience's understanding. In a world where the average attention span is just eight seconds, clarity isn't a luxury—it's a necessity.

## What Happens When Your Message Lacks Clarity?

Unclear messages can have a ripple effect on your business:

1. **Missed Opportunities**: Potential clients or investors may pass you by because they don't understand your value.
2. **Wasted Time**: Miscommunication with your team can lead to confusion, mistakes, and inefficiency.

3. **Damaged Reputation**: Inconsistent or convoluted messaging can make you seem unprofessional or untrustworthy.

## Crafting a Core Message

So, how do you achieve clarity? The answer lies in creating a core message—a single, powerful statement that captures the essence of what you offer and why it matters.

Your core message is the anchor of your communication strategy. It's the one thing you want your audience to remember about you, even if they forget everything else. Here's how to craft it:

## Step 1: Define Your Purpose

Before you can communicate effectively, you need to be clear on your own goals. Ask yourself:

- What is the primary purpose of my message?
- What action do I want my audience to take?
- How do I want them to feel?

For example, if you're launching a new product, your purpose might be to inform your audience about its benefits and encourage them to make a purchase.

## Step 2: Know Your Audience

Clarity begins with understanding who you're speaking to. What are their needs, challenges, and desires? The more you know about your audience, the better you can tailor your message to resonate with them.

Think about:

- What problems does your audience need solving?
- What language or tone will they respond to?
- What objections or concerns might they have?

For instance, if your target audience is busy professionals, your message should be concise and results-oriented, emphasizing how your solution saves time or increases productivity.

## Step 3: Focus on One Big Idea

A common mistake in communication is trying to say too much at once. The result? A message that's overwhelming and forgettable. Instead, focus on one big idea—the key takeaway you want your audience to remember.

Ask yourself:

- What is the most important thing I want to communicate?
- How can I simplify my message without losing its impact?

For example, instead of saying, “Our software offers a variety of features, including real-time analytics, seamless integration, and advanced customization options,” you might say, “Our software helps you make smarter decisions faster.”

## The Elements of a Resonant Message

Once you’ve identified your core message, it’s time to refine it. A resonant message has three key elements:

1. **Clarity:** Your message should be free of jargon, unnecessary details, and ambiguity. Use simple, straightforward language that’s easy for your audience to understand.
2. **Relevance:** Your message should address your audience’s specific needs and

challenges. It's not about what you want to say—it's about what they need to hear.

3. **Emotion:** People make decisions based on emotion, not logic. Use storytelling, analogies, or vivid imagery to create an emotional connection with your audience.

## Examples of Clear vs. Unclear Messaging

1. **Unclear Message**: "Our consulting services are designed to help businesses optimize their processes and improve their overall performance in a variety of ways."

**Clear Message**: "We help businesses streamline operations and boost profits through customized consulting solutions."

2. **Unclear Message**: "Our skincare line features natural ingredients and is designed for people who want better skin."

**Clear Message**: "Get glowing skin naturally with our plant-based skincare, crafted for busy professionals."

In each case, the clear message is focused, relevant, and speaks directly to the audience's needs.

## The Power of Repetition

Clarity isn't just about saying the right thing—it's about saying it consistently. Repetition reinforces your message and ensures it sticks.

Think about some of the most successful brands in the world. Coca-Cola, for example, doesn't just tell you they sell beverages. They consistently communicate the idea of happiness and refreshment in every ad, slogan, and campaign.

Your core message should be the thread that ties all your communication together, from your website copy to your elevator pitch.

## Practical Exercises for Achieving Clarity

1. **The One-Sentence Challenge**: Write down your core message in one sentence. If you can't, your message is too complicated.
2. **The "So What?" Test**: After crafting your message, ask, "So what?" This forces you to focus on the value and relevance of what you're saying.
3. **Audience Feedback**: Test your message on a few members of your target audience. Ask them to repeat it back to

you in their own words. If they can't, you need to simplify further.

## Conclusion: Clarity as Your Competitive Edge

In a crowded marketplace, clarity is your competitive edge. It's what turns a forgettable pitch into a compelling story, a hesitant prospect into a loyal client, and a confused audience into engaged supporters.

By crafting a core message that's clear, relevant, and emotionally resonant, you not only capture attention—you create connection and inspire action.

In the next chapter, we'll explore the empathy-driven approach to understanding your audience. After all, clarity is most effective when it speaks directly to the hearts and minds of the people you're trying to reach.

# CHAPTER 3

## The Empathy Edge – Understanding Your Audience

Communication is often seen as a one-way street: the speaker delivers a message, and the audience listens. But truly effective communication is interactive. It begins not with speaking but with listening—listening to understand the needs, desires, and emotions of your audience. Empathy is the foundation of this process.

Empathy allows you to step into the shoes of your audience, see the world from their perspective, and tailor your message to resonate with their experiences. In a business landscape where attention spans are short and competition is fierce, empathy gives you an edge. This chapter explores how to research, understand, and connect with your audience on a deeper level, ensuring your communication isn't just heard but felt.

## Why Empathy Matters in Communication

At its core, empathy is the ability to understand and share the feelings of another. In the context of communication, it's about recognizing the challenges, motivations, and emotions of your audience. Why is this important?

1. **Connection**: People are more likely to listen and respond to someone who understands their perspective. Empathy builds trust, which is essential for meaningful interactions.
2. **Relevance**: An empathetic message speaks directly to the needs and desires of your audience, making it more engaging and memorable.
3. **Action**: When your audience feels understood, they're more likely to act on your message, whether that means buying your product, supporting your initiative, or adopting your idea.

In short, empathy turns communication into a relationship rather than a transaction.

## The Three Pillars of Empathy-Driven Communication

To connect with your audience effectively, you need to focus on three key elements:

1. **Listening**: Understanding begins with active listening—not just to words but to tone, body language, and underlying emotions.
2. **Researching**: Gaining insights into your audience's demographics, psychographics, and pain points allows you to craft a message that aligns with their experiences.
3. **Responding**: Tailoring your message to reflect what you've learned demonstrates that you've truly heard and understood your audience.

## Step 1: Listen to Understand

Listening is a skill that's often overlooked in communication. Many of us listen to respond rather than to understand, focusing on what we'll say next instead of what the other person is saying. Empathy-driven communication requires a different approach:

1. **Be Present**: Give your full attention to your audience. Eliminate distractions and focus on their words, tone, and body language.
2. **Ask Open-Ended Questions**: Encourage your audience to share more about their thoughts and feelings. Questions like "What challenges are you facing?" or "How do you feel about this idea?" invite deeper insights.
3. **Reflect and Clarify**: Summarize what you've heard to ensure you understand correctly. Phrases like "So what you're saying is..." or "It sounds like you're feeling..." show that you're engaged and listening.

For example, if you're meeting with a client, instead of jumping into your sales pitch, start by asking about their biggest pain points. Listen carefully to their answers, and use that information to shape your message.

## Step 2: Research Your Audience

While listening provides real-time insights, research gives you a broader understanding of your audience. Here's how to gather valuable information:

## Demographics

Demographics provide basic information about your audience, such as age, gender, location, and income level. This data helps you understand who they are and how to communicate with them effectively.

## Psychographics

Psychographics go deeper, exploring your audience's attitudes, values, interests, and lifestyles. For example:

- What motivates them?
- What are their fears and frustrations?
- What do they value most?

## Pain Points and Challenges

Empathy-driven communication addresses problems your audience is facing. Research their pain points by:

- Conducting surveys or interviews.
- Reading reviews or testimonials.
- Engaging with them on social media or online forums.

## Examples in Action

Imagine you're a business coach targeting small business owners. Through research, you discover that your audience struggles with time management and feels overwhelmed by digital marketing. This insight allows you to frame your message around solutions to these specific challenges, making it more relevant and impactful.

## Step 3: Tailor Your Message

Once you've listened and researched, it's time to put that knowledge into action. Tailoring your message means:

1. **Speaking Their Language**: Use words and phrases your audience understands and relates to. Avoid jargon or overly complex language.
2. **Addressing Their Needs**: Highlight how your product, service, or idea solves their specific problems or fulfills their desires.
3. **Connecting Emotionally**: Stories, analogies, and visuals that reflect your audience's experiences create an emotional bond and make your message more compelling.

## Example: A Product Launch

Unempathetic Message: "Our new software has state-of-the-art features and unparalleled efficiency."

Empathy-Driven Message: "We know managing your business is overwhelming. That's why our software streamlines your workflow, saving you hours every week so you can focus on what matters most."

The empathetic version speaks directly to the audience's pain points, showing understanding and offering a solution.

## The Role of Emotional Intelligence

Empathy is closely tied to emotional intelligence (EI)—the ability to recognize, understand, and manage emotions in yourself and others. High EI enhances your ability to connect with your audience on an emotional level. Key EI skills for empathy-driven communication include:

1. **Self-Awareness**: Understanding your own biases and emotions helps you approach your audience with an open mind.
2. **Social Awareness**: Being attuned to the emotions and dynamics of your

audience allows you to adapt your message accordingly.

3. **Adaptability**: Flexibility in your communication style ensures you can meet your audience where they are.

## Overcoming Common Barriers to Empathy

Empathy-driven communication isn't always easy. Here are some common barriers and how to overcome them:

1. **Assumptions**: Don't assume you know what your audience needs—ask and listen instead.
2. **Biases**: Be aware of any preconceived notions that might cloud your understanding.
3. **Time Constraints**: Even in fast-paced situations, take a moment to consider your audience's perspective before delivering your message.

## Practical Exercises to Build Empathy

1. **Persona Development**: Create detailed profiles of your target audience,

including their demographics, psychographics, and challenges.

2. **Empathy Mapping**: Use an empathy map to explore what your audience is thinking, feeling, saying, and doing.
3. **Active Listening Practice**: During your next conversation, focus entirely on the other person's words and emotions without planning your response.

## Conclusion: The Empathy Edge

Understanding your audience isn't just a step in the communication process–it's the foundation. When you approach communication with empathy, you build trust, relevance, and emotional connection, giving your message the power to inspire action.

Empathy is your edge in a competitive marketplace. It transforms your communication from transactional to transformational, allowing you to create meaningful relationships and lasting impact.

In the next chapter, we'll explore how to harness the power of storytelling to make your message unforgettable and emotionally engaging. Because while empathy connects, stories captivate.

# CHAPTER 4

## Storytelling That Sells – Humans Are Hardwired for Stories

Stories are as old as humanity itself. Long before the written word, people shared knowledge, passed on traditions, and connected with one another through stories. Today, storytelling is just as powerful. It's a universal language that transcends cultures, resonates on an emotional level, and has the unique ability to make people feel, think, and act.

For entrepreneurs and business owners, storytelling isn't just a nice-to-have—it's a must-have. In a marketplace crowded with noise, facts, and figures, a good story can set you apart. It can transform your message from something easily forgotten into something unforgettable. This chapter explores how to harness the power of storytelling to create emotional connections, inspire your audience, and drive business success.

## The Science of Storytelling

Why do stories work so well? Neuroscience has the answer.

When we hear facts and data, only the language-processing parts of our brain are activated. But when we hear a story, multiple areas of the brain light up, including those associated with sensory experiences, emotions, and memory. In essence, our brains treat stories as if we're living them ourselves.

This is why storytelling is so effective in business communication. It allows your audience to engage with your message on a deeper level, making it more relatable and memorable.

## What Makes a Story Compelling?

Not all stories are created equal. To be effective, your story needs to resonate with your audience and inspire action. Here are the key elements of a compelling story:

1. **A Relatable Hero**: The protagonist of your story should represent your audience's struggles, desires, or aspirations. Whether it's you, a client, or a fictional character, the hero should be someone your audience can see themselves in.

2. **A Conflict or Challenge**: Every good story involves a challenge that must be overcome. This could be a problem your audience is facing or an obstacle you've helped others solve. The conflict is what keeps your audience engaged.
3. **A Resolution**: The story should end with a solution, transformation, or success. This is where you demonstrate how your product, service, or expertise can make a difference.
4. **Emotion**: Stories that evoke emotion—whether it's hope, excitement, or empathy—are more likely to be remembered and acted upon.

## The Business Case for Storytelling

Why should you use storytelling in your business? Here are three compelling reasons:

1. **Emotional Connection**: People make decisions based on emotion, not logic. A well-told story creates an emotional connection that builds trust and loyalty.
2. **Memorability**: Facts and figures are easily forgotten, but stories stick. They make your message more memorable,

ensuring your audience thinks of you when they need your product or service.

3. **Differentiation**: In a competitive marketplace, your story can set you apart. While others focus on features and benefits, you're creating a narrative that resonates and inspires.

## Types of Stories That Sell

There are many types of stories you can use in your business. Here are three of the most effective:

## 1. Origin Stories

Your origin story explains how you started your business, why you're passionate about what you do, and what drives you. This type of story helps humanize your brand and build trust.

**Example**: "When I started my business, I was struggling to balance my passion for design with the realities of running a company. I realized there were no resources for people like me—so I decided to create them. Today, I help entrepreneurs simplify their workflows so they can focus on what they love."

### 2. Customer Success Stories

These stories showcase how your product or service has transformed the lives of your customers. They demonstrate your value in a way that's relatable and inspiring.

**Example**: "One of my clients was on the verge of closing their business due to burnout. After implementing my productivity strategies, they not only regained their energy but also doubled their revenue within a year."

### 3. Visionary Stories

Visionary stories paint a picture of the future your audience can achieve with your help. They're ideal for inspiring action and creating excitement.

**Example**: "Imagine waking up every day excited about your business because you know you're making a difference. That's the reality I help my clients create."

## How to Craft Your Story

Now that you understand the elements and types of stories, let's dive into the process of crafting your own.

### Step 1: Identify Your Purpose

What do you want your story to achieve? Whether it's building trust, inspiring action, or showcasing your value, your purpose will guide your storytelling.

### Step 2: Know Your Audience

Your story should resonate with your audience's experiences, challenges, and desires. Use the insights you gained from Chapter 3 to tailor your story to their needs.

### Step 3: Outline the Structure

A classic story structure includes:

- **Beginning**: Introduce the hero and the context.
- **Middle**: Highlight the conflict or challenge.
- **End**: Show the resolution and the transformation.

### Step 4: Add Emotional Depth

Infuse your story with sensory details, vivid imagery, and emotional language. The more your audience can feel your story, the more impactful it will be.

## Step 5: Keep It Authentic

Authenticity is key to building trust. Your story doesn't have to be perfect—it just has to be real.

## Storytelling in Action

Let's look at an example of how storytelling can transform a business message:

**Without Storytelling**:

"Our software streamlines your workflow and increases efficiency."

**With Storytelling**:

"Meet Sarah, a small business owner who was overwhelmed by managing her day-to-day tasks. She was spending hours every week on manual processes, leaving little time for growth. Then she discovered our software. Within weeks, Sarah automated her workflow, saved 10 hours a week, and grew her business by 30%. Today, she's thriving—and you can too."

The second version is more engaging and memorable because it tells a story that resonates emotionally.

## Practical Exercises for Storytelling

1. **The Story Bank**: Create a "story bank" by jotting down personal experiences, client successes, and moments of transformation. This will give you a reservoir of stories to draw from.
2. **The 60-Second Test**: Practice telling your story in 60 seconds. This helps you distill it down to its most compelling elements.
3. **Feedback Loop**: Share your story with a trusted colleague or mentor and ask for feedback on its clarity, relevance, and emotional impact.

## The Impact of Storytelling

When done well, storytelling doesn't just inform—it transforms. It turns prospects into clients, customers into loyal advocates, and businesses into unforgettable brands.

Remember, your story is your superpower. It's what makes you unique, relatable, and memorable. By mastering the art of storytelling, you can create emotional connections that inspire action and drive results.

In the next chapter, we'll explore how to craft a call to action that turns your compelling stories into measurable outcomes. Because while stories captivate, actions close the deal.

# CHAPTER 5

# Speaking Their Language – Words That Resonate

Words are the building blocks of communication. They have the power to inspire, connect, and persuade. But too often, business owners and entrepreneurs fall into the trap of using complex jargon, industry-specific terms, or overly technical language that alienates their audience instead of engaging them.

The key to effective communication lies in simplicity. When your words are clear and relatable, your message becomes more accessible, impactful, and memorable. In this chapter, we'll explore how to choose words that resonate, strengthen your message, and ensure your audience feels understood.

## Why Simplicity Matters

In a world overloaded with information, people are constantly filtering what they hear and read. If your message is too complex, your audience will tune out. Simplicity doesn't mean "dumbing down" your language; it means delivering your message in a way that's easy to understand and connects emotionally.

## The Power of Plain Language

Research shows that clear and simple language is more effective at capturing attention and inspiring action. When your audience doesn't have to work hard to understand your message, they're more likely to engage with it.

For example:

- Complex: "Our innovative platform optimizes operational efficiencies and enhances user-centric functionalities."
- Simple: "Our platform makes your work easier and faster."

The simple version is easier to understand and more relatable, ensuring your message sticks.

## The Consequences of Jargon Overload

Jargon is one of the biggest barriers to effective communication. While technical terms and industry-specific language may seem impressive, they often confuse or alienate your audience.

## Why Jargon Fails

1. **It Excludes**: If your audience doesn't understand the terms you're using, they'll feel excluded and disengaged.
2. **It Creates Distance**: Jargon can make you seem out of touch or unapproachable.
3. **It Distracts**: Instead of focusing on your message, your audience spends time deciphering your words.

## The Simplicity Rule

If a 12-year-old wouldn't understand your message, it's too complex. Aim to simplify without losing the essence of what you're trying to say.

## Speaking the Language of Your Audience

To resonate with your audience, you need to use words and phrases they relate to. Here's how:

## 1. Know Your Audience

Understanding your audience's background, needs, and preferences is the first step to speaking their language. Ask yourself:

- What are their challenges and goals?
- What terms or phrases are familiar to them?
- What tone and style do they prefer?

For example, if you're speaking to a group of creative entrepreneurs, a conversational and inspiring tone may work best. If you're addressing corporate executives, a professional and concise approach might be more effective.

## 2. Mirror Their Language

Pay attention to the words and phrases your audience uses. Whether it's through surveys, social media, or conversations, listening to their language helps you align your message with their vocabulary.

For instance:

- If your audience frequently mentions "work-life balance," use that term instead of "personal and professional equilibrium."

- If they say “getting more clients,” avoid substituting it with “optimizing client acquisition strategies.”

## 3. Use Universal Language

Even if your audience spans different demographics, you can connect with them by using universal language that appeals to shared emotions, values, and experiences.

## Techniques for Clear and Relatable Language

## 1. Short Sentences and Simple Words

Long sentences and complex words can overwhelm your audience. Break your ideas into smaller, digestible pieces.

Example:

- Complex: “Incorporating innovative methodologies into your workflow can yield significant enhancements in productivity.”
- Simple: “Using new methods can make you more productive.”

## 2. Active Voice

Active voice makes your writing more direct and engaging.

Example:

- Passive: "Mistakes were made in the process."
- Active: "We made mistakes during the process."

## 3. Concrete Examples

Abstract concepts are harder to grasp. Use specific examples to illustrate your point.

Example:

- Abstract: "Our service improves efficiency."
- Concrete: "Our service saves you five hours a week by automating your invoicing."

## 4. Visual Language

Paint a picture with your words to help your audience visualize your message.

Example:

- Plain: "Our solution is effective."
- Visual: "Our solution works like a GPS, guiding you step-by-step to your goals."

## The Role of Emotion in Language

Words that evoke emotion are more likely to resonate with your audience. People don't just want to understand your message—they want to feel it.

## Emotionally Charged Words

Use words that inspire, motivate, or create a sense of urgency. For example:

- Replace "good" with "amazing."
- Replace "save money" with "unlock financial freedom."

## Storytelling and Emotion

As we discussed in Chapter 4, storytelling is a powerful way to connect emotionally. Incorporate stories into your message to make your language more engaging and memorable.

## Avoiding Common Pitfalls

### 1. Overloading with Information

Too much information can dilute your message. Focus on one key point and communicate it clearly.

### 2. Failing to Edit

Editing is essential for clear communication. Eliminate unnecessary words, simplify complex sentences, and ensure your message flows logically.

### 3. Ignoring Feedback

Seek feedback from others to ensure your language resonates. What seems clear to you may not be clear to your audience.

## Practical Exercises to Strengthen Your Message

1. **The "Grandma Test"**

Explain your message to someone outside your field, like a friend or family member. If they don't understand it, simplify your language.

2. **Word Substitution**

Review your writing or speech and replace jargon or complex words with simpler alternatives.

3. **Audience Feedback**

Share your message with a small segment of your audience and ask for feedback on its clarity and relatability.

## Real-Life Application

Let's compare two approaches to pitching a service:

**Without Relatable Language**:

"Our proprietary framework leverages cross-functional synergies to optimize stakeholder engagement."

**With Relatable Language**:

"We help teams work better together so they can achieve their goals faster."

The second version is more relatable and effective because it uses clear, everyday language.

## Conclusion: The Power of Words

Words matter. They have the power to build bridges or create barriers. By using clear, relatable language, you can strengthen your message, connect with your audience, and inspire action.

Remember, simplicity is not a sign of weakness—it's a hallmark of mastery. The more clearly you can communicate, the more effectively you can lead, influence, and grow your business.

In the next chapter, we'll dive into the art of delivering your message with confidence and authenticity, because even the most powerful words need the right delivery to make an impact.

# CHAPTER 6

# The Psychology of Communication – How to Influence and Inspire

Communication is more than words. It's an intricate dance of intention, understanding, and influence. To truly inspire action, it's essential to understand the psychological principles that drive human behavior. Why do people say "yes" to one idea and not another? What compels them to trust a brand, follow a leader, or embrace a message?

This chapter explores the psychology of communication and introduces powerful principles—such as social proof, reciprocity, and persuasion—that can help you influence and inspire your audience effectively.

## The Foundation of Influence

Influence is not about manipulation or coercion. True influence comes from understanding your audience's needs, motivations, and desires. It's about creating a message that resonates on both a rational and emotional level.

At its core, influence is built on three pillars:

1. **Trust**: Your audience must believe in you and your message.
2. **Connection**: Your message must resonate with their values, goals, or struggles.
3. **Value**: Your audience must see a clear benefit in taking action.

These pillars form the foundation of every effective communication strategy.

## Principle 1: Social Proof

Humans are inherently social creatures. We look to others for guidance, especially when making decisions. Social proof is the psychological phenomenon where people follow the actions or opinions of others, believing that those actions are correct.

## Using Social Proof in Communication

Social proof can take many forms in business communication:

- **Testimonials and Reviews**: Sharing positive feedback from satisfied clients builds credibility.
- **Case Studies**: Real-life examples of success show that others have benefited from your product or service.
- **Popularity Metrics**: Highlighting the number of customers, followers, or participants can create a sense of trust and legitimacy.

**Example**:

Instead of saying, "Our program helps businesses grow," you could say, "Over 500 businesses have grown their revenue by 50% using our program."

The second statement leverages social proof to build trust and inspire confidence.

## Principle 2: Reciprocity

Reciprocity is the natural human tendency to return a favor. When someone gives us something of value, we feel compelled to give back. In communication, this principle can be used to build goodwill and encourage action.

## Using Reciprocity in Communication

You can incorporate reciprocity into your strategy by offering value first:

- **Free Resources**: Share a free guide, webinar, or consultation.
- **Exclusive Insights**: Provide unique tips or strategies tailored to your audience's needs.
- **Unexpected Gifts**: Surprise your audience with a bonus or token of appreciation.

**Example**:

If you're promoting a service, start by offering a free toolkit or checklist. Once your audience sees the value you provide, they'll be more likely to engage with your paid offerings.

## Principle 3: The Power of Persuasion

Persuasion is about guiding your audience to see the value in your perspective. Dr. Robert Cialdini, a renowned psychologist, identified six key principles of persuasion:

1. **Reciprocity**: As discussed, people feel compelled to return favors.

2. **Commitment and Consistency**: People prefer to act in ways that align with their previous commitments.
3. **Social Proof**: The influence of others' actions.
4. **Authority**: People trust experts or those in positions of authority.
5. **Liking**: People are more likely to say "yes" to those they like or relate to.
6. **Scarcity**: Limited availability creates urgency and increases perceived value.

Let's dive deeper into how these principles can be applied to business communication.

## Persuasion in Action

### 1. Establish Authority

Position yourself as an expert in your field by sharing your credentials, experiences, or achievements. Authority builds trust and inspires confidence.

**Example**:

"As an 8-time bestselling author and communication coach, I've helped thousands of entrepreneurs craft messages that resonate."

## 2. Create Scarcity

Highlight the limited availability of your product or service to encourage prompt action.

**Example**:

"This offer is only available to the first 50 participants. Don't miss your chance to join."

## 3. Build Liking

Connect with your audience on a personal level by sharing your story or finding common ground.

**Example**:

"I understand the challenges of building a business because I've been in your shoes. That's why I'm passionate about helping entrepreneurs succeed."

## The Emotional Connection

Logic makes people think, but emotion makes them act. To inspire action, your message must appeal to your audience's emotions.

## How to Tap Into Emotion

1. **Paint a Picture of the Future**: Help your audience visualize how their life or business will improve with your solution.
2. **Address Their Pain Points**: Show empathy for their struggles and provide a clear path to overcome them.
3. **Inspire Hope and Confidence**: Focus on the positive outcomes they can achieve.

**Example**:

Instead of saying, "Our software improves efficiency," say, "Imagine reclaiming 10 hours a week to focus on what you love while our software takes care of the rest."

## Practical Strategies to Inspire Action

### 1. Ask for Small Commitments

Start by asking your audience for a small, low-risk action, such as signing up for a free resource. Once they're engaged, they'll be more likely to take bigger steps.

### 2. Use Clear Calls to Action

Your audience should know exactly what you want them to do next. Use action-oriented language that emphasizes the benefit of taking that step.

**Example**:

"Click here to start your journey to financial freedom today."

### 3. Leverage Visual and Verbal Cues

Combine powerful visuals with persuasive language to reinforce your message.

**Example**:

Use an image of a thriving entrepreneur alongside the text: "This could be you—let's make it happen."

## Practical Exercises to Strengthen Your Influence

1. **Audience Analysis**: Identify your audience's core motivations and tailor your message to meet their needs.

2. **Case Study Creation**: Develop a case study showcasing the success of someone who took the action you're promoting.
3. **Feedback Loops**: Test different messages with a small audience and analyze their responses to refine your approach.

## The Psychology of Lasting Influence

Inspiring action isn't just about getting a "yes" in the moment—it's about creating lasting influence. When you communicate with clarity, empathy, and value, you build a relationship of trust and loyalty with your audience.

As you master the psychological principles of communication, you'll find that influencing and inspiring others becomes second nature. By leveraging social proof, reciprocity, and persuasion, you can create messages that not only resonate but also drive meaningful action.

In the next chapter, we'll explore how to master the art of delivering your message with authenticity and confidence, ensuring your words make a lasting impact.

# CHAPTER 7

## Aligning Your Message Across Platforms

In today's interconnected world, your audience interacts with your brand in various ways: through social media, email newsletters, websites, speaking engagements, and more. These touchpoints create opportunities to communicate your message, build trust, and inspire action. However, if your message is inconsistent across platforms, you risk confusing or alienating your audience.

Consistency isn't just about repeating the same words or phrases—it's about delivering a unified message that reflects your values, resonates with your audience, and reinforces your brand identity. This chapter explores how to align your message across platforms and ensure that every interaction strengthens your connection with your audience.

## Why Consistency Matters

Consistency builds trust. When your audience encounters a clear and cohesive message at every touchpoint, they feel confident that they understand who you are and what you stand for. In contrast, inconsistency can create doubt or confusion.

## The Benefits of a Consistent Message

1. **Brand Recognition**: A consistent message helps your audience easily identify and remember your brand.
2. **Trust and Credibility**: Repetition of a clear message reinforces your authority and reliability.
3. **Stronger Connections**: A unified message ensures your audience feels understood, no matter where they engage with you.

Think of consistency as the thread that ties all your communication efforts together, creating a seamless and professional experience for your audience.

## Step 1: Define Your Core Message

Before aligning your message across platforms, you must first define what that message is. Your core message is the central idea or value you want your audience to associate with your brand.

## Crafting Your Core Message

1. **What Problem Do You Solve?** Identify the primary challenge your audience faces and how you address it.
2. **What Makes You Unique?** Highlight the unique value or perspective you bring to the table.
3. **What Action Do You Want?** Determine the specific action you want your audience to take, such as signing up, purchasing, or engaging.

**Example**:

Core Message: "I help entrepreneurs craft clear, compelling messages that connect with their audience, grow their business, and generate revenue."

Your core message should serve as the foundation for all your communication efforts.

## Step 2: Adapt, Don't Copy

While your core message remains constant, the way you present it should adapt to fit each platform. Different platforms have different audiences, formats, and expectations.

## Adapting Your Message Across Platforms

1. **Speaking Engagements**: Focus on storytelling and emotional connection. Use your voice and body language to bring your message to life.
2. **Social Media**: Keep it short and engaging. Use visuals, hashtags, and conversational language to capture attention.
3. **Email Marketing**: Provide value upfront. Use a clear subject line and actionable content to keep your audience engaged.
4. **Website**: Make your message front and center. Use headlines, subheadings, and call-to-action buttons to guide visitors.

**Example**:

- Speaking Engagement: "Let me share a story about how one client transformed their business with a clear message."
- Social Media Post: "Your audience deserves clarity. What's your core message? Let's find it together. 💡"
- Email: "Struggling to connect with your audience? Here's how to craft a message that resonates."

By adapting your core message to fit each platform, you ensure it remains relevant and impactful.

## Step 3: Create a Brand Voice

Your brand voice is the personality and tone of your communication. It sets the mood for how your audience perceives you and ensures a consistent experience across platforms.

## Defining Your Brand Voice

1. **Personality Traits**: Is your brand professional, friendly, inspirational, or bold? Choose 3-5 traits that reflect your values.

2. **Tone**: Decide whether your tone should be formal, conversational, enthusiastic, or empathetic.
3. **Language Style**: Determine if your language should be simple, technical, playful, or sophisticated.

### Example of Brand Voice Guidelines:

- Personality: Professional, Empowering, Empathetic
- Tone: Warm and Conversational
- Language Style: Clear, Relatable, and Motivational

Once you've defined your brand voice, apply it consistently across all communication platforms.

### Step 4: Leverage Visual Consistency

Visual elements play a critical role in reinforcing your message. A cohesive visual identity ensures your audience immediately recognizes your brand, no matter where they encounter it.

## Key Elements of Visual Consistency

1. **Logo and Colors**: Use the same logo and color palette across platforms.
2. **Typography**: Choose consistent fonts for your website, social media, and presentations.
3. **Imagery**: Maintain a consistent style for photos, graphics, and videos.

**Example**:

If your brand colors are navy blue and gold, ensure those colors appear in your social media graphics, email templates, and presentation slides.

## Step 5: Develop a Content Calendar

A content calendar helps you plan and align your message across platforms. By mapping out your content in advance, you can ensure consistency while tailoring your approach to each platform.

## Creating a Content Calendar

1. **Identify Key Themes**: Focus on 2-3 core themes that align with your message.

2. **Schedule Content**: Plan when and where you'll share each piece of content.
3. **Repurpose Content**: Adapt blog posts into social media snippets, webinar topics into email series, and so on.

**Example**:

- Week 1 Theme: "Crafting Your Core Message"
- Blog Post: "5 Steps to Find Your Core Message"
- Social Media Post: "What's one word that defines your business? Comment below!"
- Email: "Your Core Message is the Key to Growth—Here's How to Define It."

## Step 6: Monitor and Adjust

Consistency doesn't mean rigidity. As you share your message across platforms, monitor your audience's responses and adjust as needed.

## Analyzing Your Message's Effectiveness

1. **Engagement Metrics**: Track likes, shares, comments, and click-through rates.

2. **Feedback**: Pay attention to comments, reviews, and direct messages for insights.
3. **Performance Reports**: Use analytics tools to measure the success of your campaigns.

If a particular message isn't resonating, tweak your approach while staying true to your core message.

## Practical Exercises to Align Your Message

1. **Audit Your Platforms**: Review your website, social media profiles, email campaigns, and presentations to ensure they reflect your core message.
2. **Create a Messaging Guide**: Document your core message, brand voice, and visual guidelines for easy reference.
3. **Test Your Message**: Share your message with a small group of trusted individuals and ask for feedback on its clarity and consistency.

## Real-Life Application: A Case Study

Imagine you're a coach helping small businesses with brand strategy. You decide to align your message across platforms:

- **Speaking Engagements**: Share success stories of businesses you've transformed.
- **Social Media**: Post quotes like, "Your brand is your story. Tell it with confidence."
- **Emails**: Offer tips like, "3 ways to strengthen your brand message this week."
- **Website**: Highlight your core message: "Helping small businesses find their voice and stand out."

By presenting a cohesive message, you build trust and establish yourself as an authority in your field.

## Conclusion: The Power of Alignment

Aligning your message across platforms ensures that every interaction with your audience reinforces your brand and builds trust. Consistency doesn't just make your communication more effective—it makes your brand unforgettable.

In the next chapter, we'll explore how to use technology and tools to amplify your message, reach a wider audience, and measure your impact.

# CHAPTER 8

## The Revenue Connection – Turning Communication Into Sales

Good communication drives action. Whether you're speaking to potential clients, crafting a sales pitch, or engaging in a marketing campaign, your ability to communicate effectively is the key to driving revenue. But communication in sales is more than just telling people about your product or service—it's about crafting a message that resonates, addresses pain points, builds trust, and encourages a clear call to action.

In this chapter, we will explore how to turn your communication into a tool for generating sales. We'll discuss the psychology behind a persuasive sales message, key elements of an effective sales pitch, and strategies for converting prospects into loyal clients.

## Understanding the Sales Process: The Role of Communication

Before we dive into specific strategies, it's essential to understand the connection between communication and the sales process. Sales is a journey, not a single event. It starts long before the prospect expresses interest in your product and continues after the sale as you build a relationship with your clients.

## The Stages of the Sales Journey

1. **Awareness**: This is where prospects first learn about your product or service. Communication at this stage focuses on building awareness and introducing your brand.
2. **Interest**: Once they're aware of you, prospects move into the interest stage, where they begin to seek more information. Here, your communication needs to spark their curiosity and provide value.
3. **Desire**: At this point, prospects are considering the benefits your offering provides. Your communication must deepen the emotional connection and

make them believe that your solution can solve their problems.

4. **Action**: This is the moment of truth when the prospect becomes a paying client. Your communication needs to be clear, persuasive, and compelling to prompt them to take that final step.

In each of these stages, your message should be carefully crafted to guide the prospect to the next step in the journey, ultimately leading them to make a purchase.

## The Psychology of Sales Communication

Effective sales communication is deeply rooted in psychology. To connect with prospects and move them toward making a purchase, you must understand the underlying psychological triggers that influence human decision-making.

## Psychological Triggers in Sales Communication

1. **Reciprocity**: People are more likely to say "yes" when they feel they've received something first. Offering a free consultation, a valuable resource, or even a

complimentary sample can create a sense of indebtedness, making prospects more likely to convert into paying clients.

2. **Scarcity**: The principle of scarcity suggests that people place higher value on things that are perceived to be in limited supply. By highlighting limited availability or creating time-sensitive offers, you can motivate prospects to act quickly.
3. **Social Proof**: Humans tend to look to others to make decisions. By incorporating testimonials, reviews, or case studies into your sales communication, you can show prospects that others have successfully used your product or service and encourage them to follow suit.
4. **Authority**: People trust experts. Establishing yourself as an authority in your field through thought leadership, certifications, or showcasing your experience can help build trust and make your offer more compelling.
5. **Commitment and Consistency**: When prospects make a small commitment (such as subscribing to your newsletter or downloading a free resource), they are more likely to commit to a larger purchase. By encouraging small steps

and affirming their commitment, you set the stage for a larger sale.

## Crafting a Compelling Sales Message

To turn communication into sales, your message must be clear, compelling, and persuasive. But what makes a sales message effective?

## Key Components of a Sales Message

1. **Clear Problem Definition**: Identify the pain point your product or service solves. Speak directly to your prospect's needs, desires, and struggles. Show that you understand their problem.

**Example**:

"Are you tired of feeling overwhelmed with managing your business finances? Let us help you streamline your process and regain control."

2. **Offer a Solution**: Once you've defined the problem, offer your solution. Clearly explain how your product or service will solve the prospect's issue and highlight the benefits they'll gain from choosing your offering.

**Example**:

"Our easy-to-use software automates your financial tasks, saving you time and reducing the stress of managing your finances. You'll be able to focus on growing your business instead of worrying about paperwork."

3. **Build Value**: Show why your solution is the best choice. Use evidence, such as testimonials, case studies, or results, to demonstrate how your product or service has helped others achieve their goals.

**Example**:

"Over 500 small businesses have successfully used our software to save hours every week, with some reporting a 40% increase in productivity."

4. **Create Urgency**: Make sure your prospects understand that now is the best time to take action. Use scarcity and urgency to create a sense of urgency that motivates them to act.

**Example**:

"Sign up today to lock in your special rate before our prices increase next month."

5. **Strong Call to Action**: A clear call to action (CTA) tells your prospects exactly what they need to do next. It should be specific, actionable, and easy to follow.

**Example**:

"Click here to start your free trial today and see how our software can transform your business."

## Sales Pitches That Convert

A sales pitch is a vital part of your communication strategy. It's your opportunity to engage with a prospect and present your offer in a compelling way.

## Building an Effective Sales Pitch

1. **Start with a Hook**: Grab the prospect's attention with a compelling statement or question that speaks to their pain points or desires.

**Example**:

"Do you feel like your business could be doing better, but you're not sure where to start? What if I told you we could help you grow your revenue by 30% in the next three months?"

2. **Establish Trust**: Use testimonials, success stories, or your personal expertise to build credibility and make the prospect feel comfortable.

**Example**:

"As a certified business coach with over 10 years of experience, I've helped over 200 businesses improve their marketing strategies and increase sales."

3. **Present the Solution**: Focus on the benefits your product or service offers and how it can solve the prospect's problems.

**Example**:

"Our system helps businesses automate their marketing campaigns, which means you can reach more potential clients with less effort and time."

4. **Address Objections**: Anticipate potential objections and address them proactively during your pitch. This builds trust and shows that you've considered their concerns.

**Example**:

"I know you might be concerned about the upfront cost but consider how much time and money you'll save by automating your processes. The ROI will be well worth it."

5. **Close with a Strong Call to Action**: End your pitch by prompting the prospect to take action immediately.

**Example**:

"Let's set up a demo so you can see firsthand how our system works and how it can transform your business."

## Using Sales Funnels to Nurture Leads

In addition to crafting compelling sales messages and pitches, you can also leverage sales funnels to nurture leads over time. A sales funnel is a series of steps designed to guide prospects through the buyer's journey—from awareness to decision-making.

## Building a Sales Funnel

1. **Top of Funnel (TOFU)**: At the top of the funnel, your goal is to attract prospects and build awareness. This could involve content marketing, social media, or webinars.
2. **Middle of Funnel (MOFU)**: In the middle of the funnel, you'll focus on nurturing relationships and providing more value. This is where email marketing, case studies, and free resources come in.
3. **Bottom of Funnel (BOFU)**: At the bottom of the funnel, you're ready to convert

leads into customers. This is where you use strong calls to action, limited time offers, and personal sales pitches.

## Practical Strategies for Turning Communication into Sales

1. **Use Storytelling**: People remember stories, not facts. Share stories of how your product or service has helped others, making your message more relatable and memorable.
2. **Follow Up**: Don't let prospects slip through the cracks. Consistently follow up with leads through email, phone calls, or even personalized messages to keep the conversation going.
3. **Measure and Adjust**: Keep track of the effectiveness of your sales communication. Monitor open rates, click-through rates, and conversion rates, and adjust your messaging as needed.

## Conclusion: The Power of Communication in Sales

Good communication isn't just about sharing information–it's about creating connections, building trust, and inspiring action. By crafting sales messages and pitches that resonate with your audience, addressing their pain points, and offering clear solutions, you can turn communication into a powerful tool for driving revenue.

In the next chapter, we will explore how to maintain client relationships and keep your audience engaged long after the sale.

# CHAPTER 9

# Overcoming Barriers to Real Communication

Communication is the cornerstone of personal and professional success. Yet, for many people, communicating effectively remains a significant challenge. Fear of speaking, imposter syndrome, self-doubt, and other internal barriers can prevent individuals from conveying their message with clarity and confidence. In this chapter, we'll explore common barriers to real communication and offer practical techniques for overcoming them.

## The Nature of Barriers in Communication

Barriers to communication often stem from internal and external factors. These barriers can disrupt the flow of conversation and prevent people from connecting with others in a meaningful way. While external barriers, such as environmental distractions, may be temporary or beyond your control, internal barriers are much more personal. They are often tied to emotions, beliefs, and mindsets that limit your ability to communicate effectively.

## Common Internal Barriers:

1. **Fear of Speaking**: One of the most common barriers to communication is the fear of speaking in front of others, also known as glossophobia. This fear can cause physical symptoms such as trembling, sweating, or a racing heart, all of which make effective communication difficult.
2. **Imposter Syndrome**: The feeling that you're not qualified or deserving of success, despite evidence to the contrary, can hinder your confidence and prevent you from speaking up.
3. **Self-Doubt**: Self-doubt and insecurity about your abilities can cause you to second-guess your words, leading to unclear or ineffective communication.
4. **Perfectionism**: The fear of saying something wrong or not living up to expectations can lead to paralysis by analysis, causing you to overthink every word or sentence before speaking.

5. **Negative Self-Talk**: Often, we are our own worst critics. Negative self-talk—such as telling yourself that your ideas aren't valuable or that others will judge you—can prevent you from taking the first step toward effective communication.

Recognizing these barriers is the first step toward overcoming them. By understanding where your fears and doubts originate, you can develop strategies to overcome them and communicate with clarity and confidence.

## Overcoming the Fear of Speaking

The fear of speaking, whether it's in a small meeting or in front of a large audience, is a major roadblock to effective communication. Fortunately, it's a fear that can be managed and overcome with the right approach.

## Techniques for Overcoming Fear of Speaking

1. **Preparation is Key**: One of the best ways to reduce fear is to be well-prepared. Whether you're delivering a speech, a presentation, or participating in a meeting, practice can make a significant difference. Write out your

key points, rehearse them, and become familiar with the content. The more prepared you feel, the less anxious you will be.

2. **Breathe and Relax**: Deep breathing exercises can help calm the nervous system and reduce anxiety. Before speaking, take slow, deep breaths to center yourself and regain focus. In addition, progressive muscle relaxation techniques can help ease physical tension, allowing you to feel more relaxed and confident.

3. **Visualize Success**: Visualization is a powerful tool for overcoming fear. Take a moment to close your eyes and imagine yourself speaking confidently. Visualize the positive reactions from your audience and how your message is received with interest and engagement. This technique can help shift your mindset from fear to confidence.

4. **Start Small**: If the idea of speaking in front of a large group terrifies you, start small. Begin by speaking in front of trusted friends or colleagues. Gradually increase the size of your audience as you gain confidence. Each small success will build your self-assurance and reduce your fear over time.

5. **Focus on the Message, Not Yourself**: Often, fear arises from worrying about how

others perceive us. Shift your focus away from yourself and concentrate on the value of your message. Remember, your audience is more interested in what you're saying than in how you're saying it. By focusing on the message and the value it brings, you can reduce self-consciousness and anxiety.

## Conquering Imposter Syndrome

Imposter syndrome is the feeling that you don't deserve your success or that you're "faking it." It can cause you to doubt your abilities and prevent you from communicating with authority and confidence. The key to overcoming imposter syndrome is acknowledging it, reframing your mindset, and celebrating your accomplishments.

## Techniques for Overcoming Imposter Syndrome

1. **Acknowledge Your Achievements**: Imposter syndrome thrives on the belief that your success is due to luck or external factors, not your hard work or skills. Take time to reflect on your accomplishments and acknowledge the effort and expertise that led to your success. By recognizing your

contributions, you can build confidence and internal validation.

2. **Reframe Negative Thoughts**: When you experience feelings of inadequacy, reframe those thoughts. Instead of thinking, "I'm not qualified," try thinking, "I've worked hard to get here, and I have valuable insights to share." This shift in perspective can help you silence the inner critic and boost your self-confidence.
3. **Seek Support and Mentorship**: Talking to others who have experienced similar feelings can help you realize that imposter syndrome is common and not a reflection of your worth. Seek out mentors or peers who can provide encouragement and support, and who can remind you of your strengths.
4. **Embrace the Growth Mindset**: Understand that learning and growth are ongoing processes. Even if you make mistakes, it doesn't mean you're not qualified or capable. A growth mindset allows you to view challenges as opportunities for improvement, not as evidence of inadequacy.
5. **Celebrate Small Wins**: Imposter syndrome often causes individuals to dismiss their accomplishments, no matter how significant. Instead of minimizing your

achievements, take time to celebrate small wins along the way. Acknowledging your progress helps build self-esteem and encourages future success.

## Overcoming Self-Doubt and Perfectionism

Self-doubt and perfectionism often go hand-in-hand, creating a cycle of hesitation and missed opportunities. The constant fear of not measuring up or making mistakes can paralyze your ability to communicate effectively.

## Techniques for Overcoming Self-Doubt and Perfectionism

1. **Challenge Negative Beliefs**: When you experience self-doubt, take a step back and question the validity of your thoughts. Are they based on facts or assumptions? Often, self-doubt is based on unfounded fears and misconceptions. Challenge those thoughts and replace them with more realistic, positive affirmations.
2. **Accept Imperfection**: Perfectionism can be paralyzing. Understand that no one is perfect, and it's okay to make mistakes. In

fact, mistakes often provide valuable learning experiences. By embracing imperfection, you free yourself from the fear of failure and open yourself up to more authentic communication.

3. **Set Realistic Expectations**: Rather than expecting perfection, set realistic and achievable goals for your communication efforts. Aim for progress, not perfection, and give yourself credit for the steps you take, even if they're not flawless.
4. **Practice Self-Compassion**: Be kind to yourself when you make mistakes or experience setbacks. Self-compassion allows you to treat yourself with the same understanding and patience you would offer a friend. By being gentle with yourself, you reduce the pressure to be perfect and create a healthier mindset for communication.

## Building Confidence in Communication

Confidence in communication is built through practice, self-awareness, and a positive mindset. Overcoming the barriers mentioned above allows you to unlock your full potential and communicate with greater clarity, conviction, and effectiveness.

## Techniques for Building Confidence

1. **Practice, Practice, Practice**: The more you practice communication, the more comfortable and confident you'll become. Look for opportunities to speak in front of groups, whether through public speaking, leading meetings, or participating in workshops. The more you practice, the more natural communication will feel.
2. **Prepare for Success**: Preparation is a key factor in building confidence. When you are thoroughly prepared, you reduce the likelihood of stumbling or forgetting key points, which increases your self-assurance.
3. **Focus on Your Strengths**: Everyone has unique communication strengths. Whether it's your ability to tell compelling stories, explain complex ideas clearly, or engage with your audience, focus on what you do well. Highlighting your strengths boosts your confidence and helps you communicate more effectively.
4. **Visualize Positive Outcomes**: Before engaging in communication, visualize a

positive outcome. Imagine yourself speaking with confidence, your audience responding positively, and achieving your desired result. This mental rehearsal helps prime your mind for success.

## Conclusion: Unlocking Your Communication Potential

Overcoming the barriers to real communication is a continuous journey. Fear of speaking, imposter syndrome, self-doubt, and perfectionism can hold you back from reaching your full potential as a communicator. However, by using the techniques discussed in this chapter—preparing, reframing negative thoughts, practicing self-compassion, and focusing on your strengths—you can break through these barriers and communicate with greater clarity, confidence, and impact.

In the next chapter, we'll explore the importance of ongoing communication practice and how you can continue to refine your skills to achieve long-term success.

# CHAPTER 10

# Becoming a Communication Powerhouse

Success isn't built in a day—it's cultivated through consistent practice. This principle holds true in every area of life, but it is especially vital when it comes to communication. The ability to communicate clearly, effectively, and confidently is not an innate trait that you either have or don't have. Instead, it is a skill that can be developed, refined, and strengthened over time. In this chapter, we will explore how to establish daily habits and long-term strategies for continuous improvement in communication. Whether you're speaking to a team of executives or addressing an audience of hundreds, your communication ability can grow into one of your greatest assets.

## The Importance of Consistent Practice

In any skill development, consistent practice is key to mastering the craft. Communication is no different. Whether you're improving your public speaking, becoming more assertive in meetings, or simply learning to listen better, practicing daily helps you refine your approach, build confidence, and master the art of engaging others.

## Why Consistency Matters

Consistency is about cultivating habits that work to your advantage. Just like physical exercise strengthens muscles, regular practice strengthens communication skills. Over time, these practices will feel more natural, and you will see significant improvement.

Moreover, consistent practice helps you identify patterns in your communication—both strengths and weaknesses. Are you frequently interrupted during meetings? Do you struggle to make your message clear during presentations? Understanding your communication habits will allow you to work toward eliminating weaknesses while continuing to build on your strengths.

## Daily Habits for Communication Improvement

Building a powerful communication skillset begins with integrating intentional habits into your daily routine. These habits will not only help you become a more effective communicator but also increase your overall confidence when engaging with others.

## 1. Practice Active Listening

Communication is a two-way street. It's not just about how well you speak but how well you listen. Active listening is a skill that requires full attention, acknowledgment, and feedback. By practicing active listening every day, you'll become better at understanding others' needs and responding appropriately.

**How to Practice Active Listening:**

- Focus entirely on the speaker.
- Avoid interrupting or thinking about your response while the other person is talking.
- Nodding or providing brief verbal affirmations (e.g., "I see," "That's interesting") helps show you're engaged.
- After the speaker finishes, reflect back key points to ensure you understood correctly.
- Ask follow-up questions to show interest and clarity.

By engaging in active listening on a daily basis, you'll develop a deeper understanding of what others are trying to convey, making it easier for you to respond in a way that strengthens relationships and fosters collaboration.

## 2. Engage in Regular Reflection

Every day offers an opportunity to reflect on how you communicated. What went well? What could have been done differently? Reflecting on your daily interactions helps you identify patterns, areas for growth, and strengths to build upon.

**How to Practice Reflection:**

- At the end of each day, think back to key conversations and interactions.
- Ask yourself what went well and why. Was there a moment where you felt particularly confident?
- Identify areas where you might have faltered. Did you forget key points or struggle to get your message across?
- Write down specific communication goals for improvement.

Regular reflection allows you to measure your progress, learn from your experiences, and stay committed to improving your communication skills.

## 3. Set Specific Communication Goals

Setting clear, achievable goals is essential for growth. Without a plan, it's easy to fall into old patterns of ineffective communication. By setting specific goals for your communication, you can track progress, celebrate successes, and target areas of improvement.

**Examples of Communication Goals:**

- Improve clarity in presentations by organizing ideas into clear, concise points.
- Speak up in at least two meetings per week, offering suggestions or asking questions.
- Learn how to manage nerves before a speaking engagement by practicing relaxation techniques.

Writing down your goals and revisiting them regularly will keep you focused on continuous growth. With each goal you accomplish, you will gain more confidence in your ability to communicate.

## 4. Read and Expand Your Vocabulary

The more words you know, the more precisely you can communicate. Expanding your vocabulary doesn't just mean learning big words; it's about learning how to use language effectively to connect with others. Reading diverse materials, whether it's books, articles, or essays, will expose you to new ideas, different speaking styles, and effective ways to communicate.

**How to Build Your Vocabulary:**

- Read books, articles, and blogs on various subjects to familiarize yourself with different styles of communication.
- Make a habit of learning and using one new word every day in conversation.
- Keep a journal where you note down new phrases or words you find particularly impactful and try incorporating them into your daily speech.

A rich vocabulary allows you to express yourself more clearly and persuasively, leading to more effective communication overall.

## 5. Practice Public Speaking

Whether it's speaking in front of an audience or just presenting your ideas in a meeting, public speaking is a critical communication skill. Practicing public speaking regularly will improve your delivery, presence, and ability to connect with an audience.

**How to Practice Public Speaking:**

- Start by practicing in front of a mirror or recording yourself. Pay attention to your body language, tone, and pacing.
- Participate in local speaking events or join organizations like Toastmasters International to practice in front of others.
- Use feedback from trusted friends or colleagues to improve your performance.

The more you practice, the more comfortable and natural public speaking will feel, transforming you into a more confident and compelling communicator.

## Long-Term Strategies for Continuous Improvement

While daily habits are the foundation of becoming a communication powerhouse, long-term strategies ensure that your progress is sustained and that you continue to evolve as a communicator over time. These strategies are about building resilience, expanding your knowledge, and committing to long-term growth.

## 1. Seek Constructive Feedback

Constructive feedback is one of the most powerful tools for growth. To continuously improve, it's essential to seek feedback from others—whether it's a colleague, a mentor, or a friend. Feedback helps you identify blind spots and areas that require further development.

**How to Seek Feedback:**

- After a presentation or important conversation, ask someone you trust for honest feedback.
- Be open to both positive and negative comments. Constructive criticism is an opportunity for growth, not a personal attack.
- Focus on specific aspects of your communication, such as clarity, body language, or tone of voice.

By regularly seeking and acting on feedback, you ensure that your communication skills stay sharp and that you keep improving.

## 2. Stay Committed to Lifelong Learning

Communication is a dynamic skill, influenced by changing social norms, technology, and cultural shifts. To stay relevant and effective, it's important to commit to lifelong learning. Whether through workshops, online courses, or self-study, always look for ways to enhance your communication skills.

**Ways to Continue Learning:**

- Take online courses in communication, public speaking, or business writing.
- Attend seminars, conferences, or webinars to learn from experts in the field.
- Read books and articles on communication to keep up with the latest trends and techniques.

The more you invest in learning, the more equipped you will be to handle any communication challenge that comes your way.

## 3. Embrace Mentorship and Coaching

Finding a mentor or working with a communication coach can significantly accelerate your growth. A mentor or coach can provide tailored advice, support, and strategies that help you overcome obstacles and reach new levels of communication success.

**How to Work with a Mentor or Coach:**

- Choose someone who has experience in communication and who can offer practical insights.
- Be open to their suggestions and be willing to challenge yourself.
- Set clear goals with your mentor or coach and work together to achieve them.

Mentorship and coaching provide personalized guidance that can help you refine your communication skills and avoid common pitfalls.

## 4. Celebrate Your Successes

Lastly, remember to celebrate your successes along the way. It's easy to get caught up in the pursuit of perfection, but acknowledging your progress is key to staying motivated. Every time you improve a skill or achieve a goal, take a moment to celebrate.

**How to Celebrate:**

- Reflect on the goals you've achieved and how far you've come.
- Share your success with others who supported you in the process.
- Treat yourself to something special as a reward for your dedication.

Celebrating small wins reinforces the habit of continuous improvement and reminds you that communication mastery is a journey, not a destination.

## Conclusion: Your Path to Becoming a Communication Powerhouse

Becoming a communication powerhouse doesn't happen overnight. It takes dedication, consistent practice, and a commitment to lifelong growth. By cultivating daily habits such as active listening, reflection, and goal-setting, and by incorporating long-term strategies like seeking feedback and embracing mentorship, you can continue to refine your communication skills and achieve greater success. Remember, communication is an ongoing process of learning, experimenting, and improving. With patience and perseverance, you can turn communication into your superpower, unlocking opportunities for personal and professional growth.

# CONCLUSION

## Your Next Step – Transforming Words Into Action

You've journeyed through the principles, strategies, and techniques that can transform your communication from basic speaking into a powerful tool for connection, leadership, and growth. As we reach the end of this book, the key question remains: What will you do with what you've learned? Understanding the theory is only part of the equation; now it's time to take action. Words, in isolation, hold no true power—action is what breathes life into them. This final chapter is not just about reflecting on the knowledge you've gained but about translating that knowledge into tangible steps that will propel your business forward.

In this section, we will explore how to integrate these tools into your daily practice, overcome hesitation, and step into your power as a communicator. It's time to move beyond speaking and start connecting, inspiring, and leading with the clarity and confidence that will set your business apart. The transformation starts now.

## The Power of Action

Learning to communicate effectively is one of the most valuable skills you can cultivate as a business owner or entrepreneur. But knowledge alone is not enough. Communication is about bringing your ideas to life, rallying others behind your vision, and motivating people to take action. Whether it's in the form of a sale, a partnership, or a commitment to your cause, your communication must prompt action.

Action is what turns words into results. In this context, transformation comes when you take the tools you've learned throughout this book and actively apply them to your business. Consistent, intentional action is the fuel that will propel your business forward.

## Why Action Matters:

1. **Bringing Ideas to Life**: Speaking with purpose and clarity allows you to bring your ideas and vision to life. The clearer you are in your communication, the easier it is for others to understand and buy into what you're offering.
2. **Building Relationships**: Every interaction, whether it's in person, over the phone, or online, is an opportunity to build

meaningful relationships. Action requires you to listen actively, engage empathetically, and respond appropriately to others.

3. **Inspiring Confidence**: When you communicate with confidence, you inspire others to trust you, invest in you, and follow your lead. Action shows your commitment to your message and to your business's growth.

4. **Generating Revenue**: Ultimately, effective communication—paired with action—drives revenue. You can have the most compelling message, but without taking the necessary steps to share it, you will not convert interest into sales.

It's time to stop letting fear, doubt, or hesitation hold you back. The tools and strategies you've learned in this book are only as effective as your willingness to act on them. You have everything you need to create real change—now it's time to take the first step.

## Step Into Your Power as a Communicator

Now that you know how to communicate with clarity, it's time to step into your power. This means not just speaking your message, but owning it. It means standing firm in your message, no matter how challenging it may seem, and presenting yourself as the confident leader your business needs.

One of the most powerful ways to own your message is through your body language and presence. How you carry yourself in a conversation, presentation, or even an email speaks volumes about how confident you are in what you're saying. If you want to be a leader in your industry, your communication must reflect the authority and credibility you wish to project.

## How to Step Into Your Power:

1. **Own Your Message**: Speak with conviction and confidence. Believe in the value you bring to the table and let that belief shine through in your words. If you don't believe in what you're saying, it will be hard for others to believe in it, too.
2. **Align Your Words and Actions**: Make sure that your words align with your actions. Consistency between your communication and behavior builds trust and establishes your credibility as a leader.
3. **Practice Assertiveness**: Assertiveness is about being clear and confident while respecting others. It is not about being

aggressive or dominating, but about conveying your ideas and boundaries in a way that invites collaboration rather than confrontation.

4. **Embrace Vulnerability**: Sometimes, being a powerful communicator means being open and vulnerable. Showing that you don't have all the answers but are willing to learn and grow makes you more relatable and authentic.

By stepping into your power, you elevate your ability to influence, lead, and connect. When you show up with confidence, others will follow. As a business owner, this kind of leadership is crucial in attracting the right opportunities, clients, and partners. The world is waiting for your unique message—and now is the time to step into your full potential.

## Connect, Inspire, Lead

Effective communication isn't just about getting your message across; it's about connecting with your audience on a deeper level. As you learn to craft and deliver your message with clarity, you'll find that the best results come when you connect with others and inspire them to act. This connection is the foundation for building trust, which is essential for any long-term business success.

Communication that connects doesn't just inform—it resonates. It speaks to the heart of the people you're communicating with and makes them feel seen, heard, and understood. When you can inspire others through your words, you're not just conveying information; you're motivating them to take action.

## Strategies for Inspiring Action Through Communication:

1. **Share Stories that Resonate**: Stories are one of the most powerful ways to connect and inspire. When you use storytelling to share your personal experiences, challenges, and successes, your audience will be able to see themselves in your narrative, which creates an emotional connection.
2. **Use Emotional Appeal**: While facts and logic are essential, emotions are often what drive decisions. Use your communication to make people feel something—whether it's excitement, curiosity, or hope.
3. **Inspire Trust**: Trust is the cornerstone of any strong relationship. Be honest, transparent, and consistent in your communication,

and you'll inspire confidence in your audience.

4. **Call to Action**: Don't just leave your audience hanging. When you've connected with them emotionally, and inspired them with your story or message, ask them to take action. Whether it's signing up for your service, purchasing your product, or engaging with your brand, make sure you provide clear and actionable next steps.

Inspiring action through communication requires a deep understanding of what your audience needs, wants, and values. It's not enough to simply speak—your words must inspire others to take that next step toward what you have to offer.

## Watch Your Business Thrive

As you take these strategies and begin applying them, you will begin to notice a transformation in your business. The connections you build through clear, compelling communication will help you attract the right clients, partners, and opportunities. Your business will no longer be just about selling a product or service—it will be about creating a community of people who believe in your vision and want to be part of it.

Remember, growth doesn't happen overnight. The impact of your communication will compound over time. With consistent effort, you will see your business not only grow but thrive. You'll establish yourself as a trusted leader in your field, someone who inspires confidence, motivates others, and consistently gets results.

## The Transformation Starts Now

The journey toward becoming a communication powerhouse begins with one simple decision: to take action. You have the tools, the strategies, and the knowledge to turn words into action and elevate your business to new heights. As you step forward, remember that communication is not just a skill—it's a way of leading, connecting, and creating change.

The transformation you've been seeking doesn't have to wait. It starts now, with the next conversation, the next presentation, and the next opportunity to share your message. Take what you've learned, apply it with intention, and watch as your business flourishes. The world is waiting to hear from you—now is the time to speak with clarity, purpose, and confidence.

www.ingramcontent.com/pod-product-compliance
Lightning Source LLC
LaVergne TN
LVHW050917210926
848482LV00012B/477